NOAH

Penelope Shuttle lives in Cornwall. *Lyonesse* appeared from Bloodaxe Books in June 2021, and was Observer Poetry Book of the Month. *Covid/Corvid*, a pamphlet written with Alyson Hallett, was published by Broken Sleep Books, September 2021. Shuttle has received an Eric Gregory Award, and a Cholmondeley Award. *Redgrove's Wife*, (Bloodaxe Books, 2007), was shortlisted for the T S Eliot Award, and for The Forward Prize. *Lyonesse* was recently long-listed for the Laurel Prize. She is working on a new full-length collection, *History of the Child*.

Also by Penelope Shuttle

Lyonesse	(Bloodaxe, 2021)
Will you walk a little faster?	(Bloodaxe, 2017)
Unsent: New & Selected Poems 1980-2012	(Bloodaxe Books, 2012)
Sandgrain and Hourglass	(Bloodaxe, 2010)
Redgrove's Wife	(Bloodaxe, 2006)
and then A Leaf Out of His Book	(Oxford Poets/Carcanet, 1999)
Selected Poems 1980-1996	(Oxford University Press, 1998)
Building a City for Jamie	(Oxford University Press, 1996)
Taxing the Rain	(Oxford University Press, 1994)
Adventures with My Horse	(Oxford University Press, 1988)
The Lion from Rio	(Oxford University Press, 1986)
The Child-Stealer	(Oxford University Press, 1983)
The Orchard Upstairs	(Oxford University Press, 1981)

Noah

Penelope Shuttle

Broken Sleep Books

in memory of Morag Smith
fellow poet
dearest friend

ISBN: 978-1-915760-35-7

Cover designed by Aaron Kent

Edited and typeset by Aaron Kent

Broken Sleep Books Ltd
Rhydwen
Talgarreg
Ceredigion
SA44 4HB

Broken Sleep Books Ltd
Fair View
St Georges Road
Cornwall
PL26 7YH

Contents

Now Noah never ceases
except yon eight in this ark stowed
And seed that I will save
of these various beasts
Noah never ceases
(that night he begins)
Ere all were stowed and enclosed,
as the command required.
　— Chester Miracle Play Cycle

'Hastou nat herd', quod Nicholas, 'also
The sorwe of Noe with his felaweshipe
Er that he myghte brynge his wyf to shipe?
Hym hadde be levere, I dar wel undertake,
At thilke tyme, than all his wetheres blake,
That she hadde a shipe hirself allone.'
— The Miller's Tale, Chaucer, on the quarrels of Noah and his wife

Captain Noah

Noah is speaking us big iron words
before the birds become caged
before Noah the shepherd
charms both wolf and lamb

a mighty speech
of pounded measure
spoken on behalf of god
and with sorrowful élan

he's describing us
our last breaths
pointing to the nine-lives sky
dark as a billowy bowl of winter soup

Noah's wife holds her nose
observes that the Ark is the other side of hygienic
but her sons rush her down into the hold
like a convict or a trafficked one

Lady Eve

where shall we put all the besta, boss?
it seems a big ask by snivel and snort

the time of flood is at hand
Lady Eve swims merrily by

and so, cudgelling our breasts
and making grim cheer of it, we begin

following Noah's directions
eventually all sixteen thousand beasts are stowed

every creature taking rightful place
in the three-storeyed ark

even a pair of adolescent sauropods
which bible believers say
were in fact no bigger than your average bison

in go the mammals then the reptiles then the birds
all on the self-same day

the Ark wasn't always a toy
the Ark carried living cargo in its wooden womb

it was bigger than the USS Gerald Ford
may the lord's will be done

deluge

wellspring
      of seed
Noah saved
      in the brimful ark
            the wolvene
            the kyne
all the nobility of beast
the silken worm best
      of all
plus the pigs
      those pearly-queens
the diminutive-souled giraffes
the carry-castles   the heath-cats
sailing past all dangers
      the three pestilences of the reign of Edward III
      the raging-about of the water-newts from stem to stern
      the lurking places of the Semi-Saxons
until the dovene sprang up
to silence the owl and slay her stepfather not once but thrice

Madame Spider's diary (extract)

we creatures file aboard
we look sharp
overseers with whips command us

who are we to judge grand matters
we animals of muckle tongue
and fit-for-purpose claws

when towns are five-fathom deep
name-stones under the whale's spouting way?

Noah will voyage us
he say
to safety in Syria
or Iran or Armenia

our days afloat
are simple enchantments of the bear
opportunistic leopard's coat of many colours

elephant proud of holding his breath longest
the pangolin neat as a Lutheran
my own spun-silk line of duty

beaten breast of our lost dens
vespertinal frog's croak-song
porcupine's quilly rattle

our nights,
a biff of firefly
big-eyed lemur
and crepuscular rabbit

Noah decrees
male and female animals be segregated
by rows of stakes
so no young
may be forged on board

this enrages the screamy lusty monkeys
cavorting like comets in an air

god's sorcerous diamonds
light up the dim ark
with swirls and hummocks of holy electricity

but even thus illuminated
learnéd Noah sighs
and the sons of Noah ponder the quick-souled herds
left to perish un-hunted

all night Noah bloweth blood from his heart
he will not sleep a winklette
till Ark descends on Ararat

nor will (for love of him) neither raven nor dove

two swamp deer
of Kaziranga
two Javan Rhinos
two Seychelles-Sheath-tailed-Bats
Nicobar Shrew
Elvira Rat
Tenkile

firebird

Noah:	wait what?
Phoenix:	
Noah:	no way
Phoenix:	is it my tail? is that the problem?

sparks fly up
from the fiery feathers
as the bird displays his majestic self

Noah:	well yes
Phoenix:	but the flood
Noah:	
Phoenix:	but *the flood*
Noah:	
Phoenix:	
Noah:	(wavering) just the one of you? no mister no missus?
Phoenix:	Just me 😞
Noah:	and what's that?
Phoenix:	um oh that my nest of spices
Noah:	
Phoenix;	bit famous, my nest
Noah:	
Phoenix:	(preens)
Noah:	how does it work?
Phoenix:	
Noah:	really?
Phoenix:	yeah
Noah:	
Phoenix:	only iron will kill the phoenix
Noah:	is that a fact?
Phoenix:	

Noah:	ok fine hop on board
Phoenix:	thanks boss 😐
Noah:	
Noah:	and obey the fire regs *bird* if you *pleeze*
Noah:	
Phoenix:	(swaggers up gangplank)

Noah's Domain, or Zooming-in on the Ark

the ants make it very clear they expect cake
the nightingales beat their wings against the bars

the little early horses are too early for Picasso
and the unicorns' luck runs out also

one of the bears holds an atlas open
at the map of Russia –

swarthy forests, sprawling taigas,
silty Lake Nero, dozens of ice-bound rivers,
thirteen seas, and a few bear-gardens

the camels give Noah a taste of his own medicine
that sombre Vagaland raven keeps chacking away

the voles are studying from home, the hodge-podgy tapirs
flaunt their tear-shaped bodies, the male less successfully

a Hawaiian monk seal argues the odds with a shelly gastropod
the zebras still consider themselves to be *regal beasts*

high dudgeon rain goes on falling for years
the nightingales beat their wings against the bars

Noah slips a charm-bottle of elephant tears
into the pocket of his foal-skin robe (don't ask)

the wolves are becoming impatient,
they can go for a week without eating, okay, but...

the pythons are nobody's pets, the squirrels
want a divorce, the fire-bellied toads are fine

but why, they wonder, are the dogs so friendly?
the pangolins are still praying, and the plague skinks

will be removed from New Zealand's Wild Life Act in 2010 –
the future has Noah hooked by the heel

scenes from the ark (i)

Noah addresses the wolfhounds
on behalf of the Ark

do not fear
nothing will spoil your sport

where is the Giraffstrich? where is the Zebril?
whispers Japheth
unto his brothers Ham and Shem
shit shit shit we've forgotten them!
Ssh
says Ham
don't tell the Old Man

the eel
is a marvellous divinity
whispers Mrs Noah
to her favourite grandson

Noah's notes (preliminary)

there's meaning in the various colours of doves
the blood of a he-goat is so hot it can dissolve diamonds

the spider is an aerial worm that feeds on air
a drink made from the tears of a stag cures heartache

bees are the very smallest of birds, born from the bodies of oxen
the cat is a shadow animal, the bible has never believed in cats

the eagle will not converse with falconers
but a she-wolf will take communion from a priest

the blue-eyed phoenix lives on a diet of crisps
hunting dogs are just as beautiful as the tallest medieval horses, the destriers,

or the soul when it is first spied as *some tiny thing, a maggot or a grub:*
when the starling speaks in French, you must listen

the hare may not always be a Christian
the moth found on a young boy's kimono sleeve brings sorrow

hawks stare at one another without moving their eyes,
this is how their young are conceived

the dragonfly never stops working on the twelve volumes of his memoirs
the pig takes mercy on the vineyard, and is the world's best wet-nurse

the he-wolf must be tricked into sleep, then bound
with a rope made from the sound of an ant's footfall,

the breath of a fish and the spittle of a bird
the snake is the best doll-maker you could ever wish for

the elephant! he takes up so much room, he won't tolerate the crocodile
he's so wise, how can I forbid him?

the three-toed sloth is nothing but a bundle of leaves,
and so is the brown-throated sloth

with her iron jaw and massive clitoris
the beauteous hyena is no more and no less than a Queen

The lion is the strangest of messengers, with his Tsar's face, the chakra of
          his tail
give him your full compliance

the swan bids the rain leave off with a swirl of her meekly-shaped wings
the oriole is an unimportant bird but proud as a hornet

the winter-sleeper ignores the moon, and the two little toads
only the mouse comes in with the blessing of god

Archa Noah

the pseudo-archaeologists have been searching
for the Ark since 339 C.E

even though there's no sign of a flood
in the geological record

the Ark   tevat tubbû
bigger than Caligula's giant ship

the pseudo-archaeologists maintain
the bones of Adam were brought on board
        (citation needed)

Archa Noah
no sky sails

some say angels drove the beasts in
not Noah

tooth-billed pigeon
south china tiger
cross river gorilla
gerb's mouse lemur
red wolf
Asian unicorn

Noah's Arche

day one hundred

as the wateriness of the world continued
supplies of apricots or Armenian apples got lower

spiders studied their Breviaries of Health
full of old English advice

while the supersaliency of the rut-starved elephants
set the boat a'rockin

the wolf-greyhound nipped Noah's ankle,
the best philosophy that wise beast knew

the weasel practiced her fine court-hand
the night-raven was on tenterhooks all the time

but everyone spoilt the little lamb

rain hung its pearly garlands everywhere
as if for a young girl's funeral

the snail crept over his delightfully-illustrated prayer book
The Arche ploughed on like Leander

Men of Troy, said the circling whale, trust not in The Horse

Noah's wife had a rose cheek
her sons were favoured into Latin by the alchemists

the dilling pig coughed quietly in his stinky pen
and the rabbits gave up democracy in favour of government by demons

bear sported a half-moon eye patch
the lark enjoyed a gobbet-royal

a dreamy louse raised Hymen's torch
the sloths did nothing at all

the lioness roared her lore spell
and the paradise tree-snake took notes (kind-of)

in that Arche three hundred cubits long
no creature could abide the half-wit polecat

      all day long Noah gazed out over the Marinorama
      oh to be mocked by a mermaid! to know the colour of her
            keen eyes!

      and the name of Noah's mother?
                          unrecorded

Noah and God: a conversation

cat is the obscurer
says God

the bee is creativity
says Noah

wolf is responsibility
says God
& panther is harmony

the bear is generosity
says Noah

dog is inhibition
& the whale is my prophet
snaps God

shark is the dreamer
says Noah

& frog the mystic
adds God quickly

scorpion is song
says Noah

the dolphin is nurture
sighs God

the butterfly is sexuality
& ram is the activist
says Noah

the goat is beauty
hisses God

turtle is the martyr
says Noah

God smiles
yes my boy!
turtle *is* the martyr

Noah Theatre

Now let the Water-Carriers come forth
to perform the play of Noah and the Fludde
Let them mum how *"The flood comes in fleeting fast;*
On every side it spreadeth full fare;
Let them play the carrying in of provisions
and the entry of the animals, bears and ants,
monkeys, mice and marmosets, etc.
Let he who plays Noah with beard of goosequills shout loudly –
For fear of drowning I am agast; Good gossip, let us draw near.
Let he who playeth Noah's Wife mock all women
gossiping in bonnet and shawl
boozing and making merry with her friends
spurning the saviour Ark
and let he who plays Shem also demean all women
as on Father Noah's orders
he seizes his mother with no respect and carries her raging
(how we all laugh) into the Ark
forcing her from her home and all she holds dear and familiar,
her household, her kitchen clean as a knife blade,
her embroidered linen, vegetable beds ready for harvest,
tearing her away on a mere promise from god
who has never spoken a word to her,
taken into exile because of a stupid hunch her old man had about the weather.

That she hadde a shipe hirself allone

I want another ark
with a drawing-room
and a fernery
no smelly animals
and the complete absence of Noah

                            says Emzara

I want an ark crowded
with candle-fingered demons
Christmas Day vampires and fang-toothed virgins
an ark flying to high heaven
under the wing of the chaffinch
and a pilot
who doesn't care a fig for Ararat

                            says Emzara

shooting the breeze
in my zephyr-zeppelin
I'll be blest
as the Dryad of the Ankerwycke Yew
who, hidden in her gloomy needled canopy,
watched Henry propose to the fated Boleyne maid

                            says Emzara

Noah's Wyf

the bible refuses
to name you

but a text
excluded from
The Book of Jubilees 160-150 B.C.

tells us
you are called
Emzara

who are we
if not given
the merit of our name?

scenes from the ark (ii)

I use every spice in the Ark's kitchen
to make my simnel cake
says Mrs Noah
but I would not have my sons swallowed-up in it
I would not weep them into its rich crust   let famine come or come not

This Ark is intolerable
huffle the Taoist camels
but the talented tigers
feel things could be worse
they're already planning Tigers.org.

my cubs are down for Eton, you know!
snarls Lion
as Noah backs away
from the most solar beast of all

family life

Shem, Ham and Japheth
side with sun
moon and stars

sons who'll owe their lives
to the boon
of light tipped over
our pardoned earth

sons who bring Noah
the ready cup of broth
a dose of aardwolf spit and valerian

(heard ye his wild psalming in spell-time of night?)

Noah hun drink this calmdown cup
of whitherso and why
brewed by your serious sons

ark builders who bring you back to yourself
whenever you get lost in the holy of holies
while your three daughters-in-law
sell your shoes to the air

splish splash
hoist your spirits sky-high
on a rattly rope of cobra fangs
plait your beard like a bus driver's and fix it with a loom band

trim those backsliding toenails
tazer you with kisses from here to Mount Ararat
as is writ in the Book of Jubilees

on his five-hundredth birthday

Noah prays
to chestnut-shouldered bush sparrow
and reclusive rain spider

to earthwolf
dangerous only to termites

to snow-leopard
soon to be no more than a crossword clue

to whooping crane
pondering her last will and testament

pray for me Lord Lion
pray for us Holy Ghost Koala

amen amen
say melancholy panda
bandicoot and chinchilla

maybe maybe
say Barbary stag and desert tortoise

second father of the human race

in Noah's cosy cabin
two field mice run free
nibbling crumbs as they please
or sneaking up Noah's sleeve

he dozes by the stove
as the Ark bobbles along
till God comes to his senses
and bids the deluge be gone

Noah's vineyard

night after night
Noah tests his nerve
with prayer and booze
his drunk sermons
weaving him
round the cacophonous ark
where a thorn
can't tempt him
nor a soothsayer read his mind

every morning his sons
undo his swaddling bands
wipe his chops
joke away his hangover
silly old man!
button him into new raiment
for the sober sake of the earth

although the text of the play is lost

anno
1485

To the minstrels, 6 d.

To Noah and his wife, 1s. 6d.

To Robert Brown playing God, 6 d.

To the Ship-child, 1 d.

To a shipwright for clinking Noah's ship, one day, 7 d.

22 kids for shoring Noah's ship, 2 d.

To a man clearing away the snow, 1 d.

Straw for Noah and his children, 2 d.

Mass, bellman, torches, minstrels, garlands etc, 6 s.

For mending the ship, 2 d.

To Noah for playing, 1 s.

To straw and grease for wheels, ¼ d.

To the waits for going about with the ship, 6 d.

1494

To Thomas Sawyr playing God, 10 d.

To Jenkin Smith playing Noah, 1 s.

To Noah's wife, 8 d.

The clerk and his children, 1 s. 6 d.

To the players of Barton, 8 d.

For a gallon of wine, 8 d.

For three skins for Noah's coat, making it, and a rope to hang the ship in the kirk, 7 s.

To dighting and gilding St John's head, painting two tabernackles, beautifying the boat, 7 s. 2 d.

Making Noah's ship, £5. 8 s.

Two wrights a day and a half, 1 s. 6 d.

A halser (i.e. hawser) 4 stone weight, 4 s. 8 d.

Rigging Noah's ship, 8 d.

the wife of Ham

St Hippolytus (d.235 AD)
also recounts a quaint legend
concerning
the wife of Ham:

God instructed Noah
to kill the first person
unlucky enough to point out
that the deluge had begun

Ham's wife
was in her kitchen
baking bread
when water spurted from the oven

the deluge is here!

hearing Nahlab scream
God
at once cancelled
his former command
lest Noah destroy his own daughter-in-law
(obviously a favourite of God's)

well known locally...

have you ever visited
Trengwainton
near Penzance?

this fine house was built
by Sir Rose Price
around 1820
including
five brick-walled gardens
which for reasons unknown
he insisted be designed
to the dimensions
of Noah's Ark
 (50 x 300 biblical cubits)

and strolling around
these west-facing gardens today
or observing from the platform
thoughtfully provided
by the National Trust
you can discover
the vast size of the Ark
and amuse yourself
trying (in your mind) to fit all the animals in

so thank you
Sir Rose Price
eccentric
and plantation-owner
and (I'm guessing) a bit of a Noah yourself

(a rainbow would be good now
but the sky doesn't oblige)

Noah as Breadwright

Bread has history, says Noah, it comes from the time of incorrect maps,
steppe mammoths, oliphaunts, were-hounds of the Pharaoh,

as we know from the swan's correct reading of the Testament,
and from the saints who seldom marched home laughing.

Bread is fire's classmate and tutor to the fortune cookie.
Other experts tell us of bread from the time of the Neolithic.

Bread's reward is the glee of appetite, says Noah,
turning in his bed or berth, learning the un-roomy space off by heart.

Bread is a treasure, says Noah,
be it bread baked by accident, or wise-laid in the fresh-ploughed furrow,

blessed mote thou be,
or carried with ritual care into the fogou to be offered
to the silent chthonic gods by a man whose name will grow into a proverb.

(And the father of sliced bread
would still like to say a word or two, please, if possible, adds Noah.)

An Sorrowfulle Account

An Ape there dwelt
within the Ark,
more fit for Kirk
than cabin stark.

This Cloistered Ape
of mien grave
to Philosophie and such
did give his days.

He pondered wise
upon the stars,
inwardly did discourse,
and probe his Amaze.

Alone of the Beasts
did he embrace Prisoning
and daily went contentedly
about his Visioning:

through dog-days
and through doldrum,
Kraken menace,
cyclone and storm,

he bent his Mind
to matters rare;
to question him
none but Noah did dare,

and Solitude,
alien to his kind,
this Ape embraced
with joy unconfined,

for deep in his heart
he had vowed
this Voyage to regard
not as mere jaunt,

but as Retreat
dedicate by him
to Subtile Reasoning
and Cogitation compleat,

in happy Thraldom
to theologic problem.
Aye, Philosophie's bite
was his unwearied Delight

until A Morning comes
when his Concentration wavers.
Hark, what is that sound?
His brow grows graver.

Within his humble Cell
he marks a change
most Unsublime,
the knuckle-rap of rain

on Ark's framework
quietens to caress,
the roaring Deluge
is now mere Drizzle,

Cessation awful
of that raging rain,
and upon the Ocean
a fearsome lack of Motion.

He pounds a fist
upon his chest!
His sanctuary
is compromised!

The Ark roars
with emotion unstable,
as Ox and Oryx
bray out in happy Babel.

But our Sage
is full of deep appal,
turning anguishéd visage
to caulkéd wall,

mourning his Life
of studious Seclusion,
and dreading reunion
with his bossy Spouse.

Alas, poor Ape,
your fate is hard.
Your Treatise
now you must discard.

The tallest tree
will not ensure solitary rumination,
nor fend him off
from his noisy Progeny.

Noah alone
was his true equal.
It doesn't do to think about
our Ape's unfortunate sequel.

exodus

(a sestude)

when the animals leave the ark
in a noisy joyous rout
they leave without a backward glance
without a thank you to Noah

they claim what is theirs
the earth
always turning
the other cheek

our earth
the queen of planets
or who knows? a charred warning
to any who care to take note

nudging through our galaxy
in their alien spacecrafts

Footnotes

p 7:   **Lady Eve:** besta: Kernewek for animals.
         The USS Gerald Ford is the largest aircraft carrier in the world.

p 13:   **Noah's Domain, or Zooming-in on the Ark:** Plague skinks
were introduced into New Zealand from Australia and are now
Unwanted Organisms under the Biosecurity Act 1993, New Zealand.
It is illegal to knowingly move, spread, release, breed, display or
sell plague skinks without permission from MAF Biosecurity, New
Zealand. See the Department of Conservation website (www.doc.
govt.nz/plagueskinks) or the MAF Biosecurity New Zealand website
(www.biosecurity.govt.nz/pests/rainbow-skink)

p 14:   **scenes from the ark (i):** the Giraffstrich, the Zebril: two
of the fantastic animal costumes designed by Gerald Scarfe for the
Los Angeles Opera's production of *The Magic Flute* in 1993.

P 17:   **Archa Noah:** tevat: biblical Hebrew for ark; tubbû:
Aramaic (?) for ark.

p 21:   **Noah and God:** a conversation: some details in the above
are adapted from The Lunar Tree Calendar.

p: 22:   **Noah Theatre:** The medieval Chester play of Noah relates
the story of Noah and the Great Flood, traditionally acted by the
Drawers of Dee (watercarriers). In it, Noah and his sons load up the
provisions and the animals while his wife gossips with the neighbours.
Noah urges her to hurry aboard, *"The flood comes in fleeting fast; On
every side it spreadeth full fare; For fear of drowning I am agast; Good
gossip, let us draw near"*. However, Noah's wife keeps on drinking and
gossiping until, eventually, the sons carry her onto the ark by force.

p 23: *That she hadde a shipe hirself allone:* The Ankerwycke Yew Tree is believed to be 2,500 years old and stands close to the ruins of St Mary's Priory, a twelfth century Benedictine nunnery near Wraysbury, by the River Thames and the meadows of Runnymede. Legend says that Henry the Eighth proposed to Anne Boleyne under this ancient yew. Anne Boleyne's name is spelt in several variants, as was the contemporary mode.

p 30: **although the text of the play is lost:** This is a found poem, taken from the records of the Trinity House Guild of Master Mariners and Pilots at Hull. The maritime associations of the play of Noah made it a special favourite with this Guild; and some of their records of payments for the acting and equipment are preserved, although the text of their play is lost. (Chambers, *Mediaeval Stage*, vol.ii, pp.370-1).

p 33: A Walk in the Park, Creation Magazine 37 (3): 21, July 2015

p 37: sestude: a poetic form of 62 words (excluding the title) invented by John Simmons of the 26 Collective, for their project *Twenty Six Treasures* based upon artefacts in The National Museum of Scotland.

Noah's Notes (Preliminary): Behind the Poem

My poem imagines Noah on duty by the Ark's door as the animals enter. He makes notes about each of the creatures. His notes are preliminary, however. How much more time will he spend, I wonder, studying (like a biblical David Attenborough) the life-style of the creatures penned in the Ark as it sails along the flood?

I'm a secular person but of a generation that learned bible stories at school. The magic and richness of these stories has stayed with me as mythology, not theology. I was pleased to find old Noah step into my poem. I see him as played by John Houston. Many animal qualities in the poem are invented, but some are adapted from old bestiaries, and a scurry around world mythologies. I am indebted to poet Alyson Hallett, for information about the female hyena.

Over the past eighteen months I have been reading various poems translated from the Anglo-Saxon, and pootling about through some Old English poems and tracts. I found several long-forgotten Old English dictionaries belonging to my late husband Peter Redgrove. I studied these in a barefoot kind of way. Some of that strange and mysterious vocabulary has found its way into recent poems. A wish to write about animals sprang from a reading of an old account of Noah and The Deluge.

> 'Noah never ceases
> (that night he begins)
> Ere all were stowed and enclosed,
> as the command required.'

Noah's Notes began as a handwritten draft, using couplets and longish lines. And this form didn't change (although a poem's form often does change as I re-write). When I'd typed up my first version I began adding creature after creature, writing directly on to the screen. Sometimes a poem must be hunted down and/or coaxed into being, but this poem arrived in a rush, as if eager to be made. Poets will know the rare exhilaration of this.

After that second draft, I made several handwritten emendations to the printout, showed the poem to a couple of poet-friends, made further adjustments, and *et voila* (or its equivalent in Aramaic) the Noah poem arrived at the place where it is now.

The above note was first published on the website of *The Poetry Society* in their series *Behind the Poem*. My poem, *Noah's Notes (Preliminary)* appeared in *The Poetry Review*, Winter, 2016, Vol.106, No.4. This poem was the first of my Noah sequence to be written.

Penelope Shuttle
23/07/2023

Acknowledgements

Acknowledgements are due to the editors of the following publications in which some of these poems first appeared: *Magma; MMU (pandemic blog); The Manhattan Review; Poetry Review; The Dark Horse.*

My thanks to Katrina Naomi, for her comments on Noah as a work-in-progress.

Thanks also to the members of the Falmouth Poetry Group, especially Caroline Carver, Rosie Haddon, Gary Mathews, Roz Quillan-Chandler, and Morag Smith.

LAY OUT 2 OF EACH OF YOUR UNREST